# WELCOME TO MY COUNTRY

# Welcome to IRAN

FRANKLIN WATTS
LONDON•SYDNEY

This edition first published in 2005 by
Franklin Watts
338 Euston Road
London NW1 3BH

Reprinted 2006

This edition is published for sale only in the United Kingdom & Eire.

© Marshall Cavendish International (Asia) Pte Ltd 2005
Originated and designed by Times Editions–Marshall Cavendish
an imprint of Marshall Cavendish International (Asia) Pte Ltd
A member of the Times Publishing Group
Times Centre, 1 New Industrial Road
Singapore 536196

Written by: Dora Yip & Maria O'Shea
Editor: Melvin Neo
Designer: Benson Tan
Picture researchers: Thomas Khoo and Joshua Ang

A CIP catalogue record for this book
is available from the British Library.

ISBN-10: 0 7496 6014 7
ISBN-13: 978 0 7496 6014 7

Printed in Malaysia

Franklin Watts is a division of Hachette Children's Books.

**PICTURE CREDITS**
Archive Photos: 16
Art Directors & TRIP Photographic Library:
    7, 8, 9 (both), 10, 15 (top), 18, 22, 27, 28,
    29, 31, 38, 39, 40
Focus Team – Italy: 45
HBL Network Photo Agency: 19, 34, 36, 37
The Hutchison Library: 2, 25
Earl Kowall: 1, 3 (bottom), 4, 6, 17, 26, 32, 41
Nazima Kowall: cover, 3 (centre), 5, 20, 21,
    23, 24, 30, 33
North Wind Picture Archives: 11
Christine Osborne Pictures: 3 (top), 35
Maria O'Shea: 44 (both)
Topham Picturepoint: 14, 15 (bottom)
Vision Photo Agency: 12, 13

Digital Scanning by Superskill Graphics Pte Ltd

# Contents

Words that appear in the glossary are printed in **boldface** type the first time they occur in the text.

# Welcome to Iran!

Present-day Iran was officially named the Islamic Republic of Iran in 1979. Although Iran is a young nation, its history dates back thousands of years. It was once the centre of the powerful Persian Empire from 550–330 B.C. Let's visit Iran and learn about its history and its people!

**Opposite:** Some villages in Iran were built between the second and seventh centuries.

**Below:** Royal Square, in the city of Esfahan, is one of the largest town squares in the world.

## The Flag of Iran

The Iranian flag has green, white and red bands. Green represents Islam. White stands for peace. Red recognises the courage and loyalty of Iran's people. The red **emblem** on the white band is Iran's national symbol.

# The Land

With an area of 1,648,000 square kilometres, Iran is almost seven times bigger than Britain. Deserts cover much of the country's central and eastern areas.

Except along the coasts, Iran lies on a **plateau**. An **elevation** of 1,219 metres makes this country one of the highest in the world.

**Below:**
The snow-capped Zagros Mountains separate Iran from the country of Iraq.

6

Three mountain ranges cut across the Iranian plateau. The Markazi range stretches from northwest to southeast. The Zagros range is in the west and southwest. The Elburz Mountains in the north contain Iran's highest peak, Mount Damavand, at 5,671 metres. The Caspian Sea which is the largest lake in the world lies directly north of the Elburz Mountains.

**Above:**
**Flamingos wade in Iran's coastal waters near the Persian Gulf.**

## Climate

Northwestern and western Iran have four seasons, including a very cold winter. During winter, temperatures can be as low as -37° Celsius. Southern and eastern Iran have only two seasons — a hot summer and a mild, rainy winter. The provinces along the Caspian Sea have a **subtropical** climate. The Elburz Mountains trap humidity in this area.

**Above:** Houses in the hottest parts of Iran are designed to stay cool inside. The tall towers on their rooftops have openings to catch outside breezes. This air flows down to the basement, where a pool or stream cools it. The cool air then **circulates** all through the house.

# Plants and Animals

Due to its climate and high altitude, Iran does not have much plant life. Most of its forests are in the humid Caspian region, where oak, ash, elm and beech trees grow. Smaller, shrub-like trees grow in some of the drier areas. Slender poplars are the most common trees in Iran.

Iran has many areas that are not suitable for people to live in, so wild animals have made homes in them. These animals include bears, lynxes, leopards, jackals, hyenas and wolves.

**Above:** Iranian pomegranates are believed to be the reddest and tastiest in the world. People in Iran use all parts of the pomegranate tree, either for food, to make dye or for medicine.

**Left:** The deserts of Iran are home to many reptiles, including the rare pygmy gecko (*Tropiocolotes latifi*).

# History

**Archaeologists** have found signs of human life in the Zagros Mountains dating back to 100,000 B.C. By about 6000 B.C., settlers and farmers lived throughout the Iranian plateau.

Around 2500 B.C., the Elamites living on the Khuzestan plains set up a **feudal** system of government that lasted until the sixth century B.C. By then, the Medes and the Parsua, or Persians, had taken over Iran.

**Left:** The tomb of Persian king Cyrus the Great is in Pasargadae, which is located in southwestern Iran. Cyrus made Pasargadae the capital of the Persian Empire because it was near the place where his army had defeated the Medes.

# The Persian Empire

In the mid-sixth century B.C., the Persians, led by King Cyrus II, defeated the Medes and created a vast empire. At its peak, the Persian Empire included Egypt, Central Asia, northern India and the Ionian Greek lands.

The Persian Empire ended when Greek ruler Alexander the Great conquered Persepolis in 330 B.C. In A.D. 651, Persia fell to the Arabs, who ruled until the thirteenth century.

**Above:** In 479 B.C., the Greek (*right*) and Persian (*left*) armies fought the Battle of Plataea. Alexander the Great admired the skill and techniques of the Persian army so much that he trained Greek troops to fight the same way.

# From Empires to Revolutions

Although Mongol invasions in the 1200s destroyed much of the Persian culture, Shah Abbas I of the Safavid **dynasty** was able to reunite Persia's kingdoms in the sixteenth century. Abbas' successors, however, could not stop the Ottoman Turks and other invaders from conquering many parts of the country. By 1900, Persia had been reduced to approximately the size it is today.

**Above:** Shah Abbas the Great ruled Persia from 1588 to 1629. He was a wise ruler, and, during his reign, the country regained some of its lost glory.

In 1921, a young army officer named Reza Khan took control of Iran's armed forces. In 1925, Reza Khan became Reza Shah Pahlavi, **sovereign** ruler of Iran. The reforms made during his rule were very unpopular, especially with Muslim religious leaders.

Reforms made by his successor, Muhammad Reza Shah Pahlavi, who was his son, were not widely accepted either. Some of Muhammad Reza

Shah Pahlavi's social and economic changes became known as the "White Revolution". These reforms included redistributing land and allowing women more freedom.

**Left:** Muhammad Reza Shah Pahlavi became Iran's ruler in 1941, but his **coronation** was not held until 1967. The shah did not want the crown until after he had restored stability and prosperity in the country.

**Left:** In 1979, troops supporting Muhammad Reza Shah Pahlavi entered the city of Esfahan to stop Iranian rebels. Many of the troops' armoured vehicles were covered with portraits of the royal family.

# The 1978–1979 Revolution

Iranians revolted against the shah's government in 1978, and on 1 April 1979, rebel leader Ruhollah (Ayatollah) Khomeini established the Islamic Republic of Iran. Many Iranians who opposed Khomeini's government were **persecuted** or killed.

With Iran in a state of political unrest, neighbouring Iraq tried to reclaim parts of southwestern Iran. The Iranians fought back, waging a war that lasted ten years and claimed a million lives. Iraq withdrew its troops in 1990.

# Cyrus the Great (c. 590/580–529 B.C.)

While Cyrus II was king of Persia, he established an empire that stretched from Central Asia to Egypt. He was a strong and wise ruler.

# Muhammad Reza Shah Pahlavi (1919–1980)

The son of Reza Shah Pahlavi, Muhammad Reza Shah Pahlavi became Iran's sovereign leader in 1941. His **autocratic** rule led to the 1978–1979 revolution, which forced him into **exile**.

**Muhammad Reza Shah Pahlavi**

# Ruhollah Khomeini (c. 1900–1989)

Muslim scholar Ruhollah Khomeini was one of Iran's most influential religious leaders. He was against Muhammad Reza Shah Pahlavi and convinced Iranians to rebel. Under Khomeini's leadership, Iran followed strict Islamic laws.

**Ruhollah Khomeini**

# Government and the Economy

## Government and Administration

Iran is an Islamic country ruled by a supreme spiritual leader, or *faqih*. The faqih makes sure the country is governed according to Islamic laws. The current faqih is Ayatollah Ali Hoseini-Khamenei.

**Above:** Muhammad Khatami was elected president of Iran in 1997. He has worked to improve relations with the West.

Iran's president, who is elected to a four-year term, is the head of state. The president chooses a cabinet of twenty-four ministers. The *Majlis*, or the Islamic Consultative Assembly, passes laws and makes economic decisions. The Council of Guardians, which is a group of twelve Islamic judges and scholars, supervises elections and makes sure that all laws follow Islamic beliefs.

Each of Iran's twenty-eight provinces has a governor-general, and each city elects a mayor.

## The Legal System

Iranian laws are based on the Qur'an, which is the holy book of Islam. Other instructions come from the Hadith, which contains teachings of the prophet Muhammad. Iran's legal system has levels of courts ranging from civil courts to a Supreme Court. Since Iranian courts follow Islamic laws, judges act without **juries**.

**Below:** The Elburz Mountains tower over the city of Tehran, which is the capital of Iran.

17

# The Economy

Iran's economy has depended on oil, the country's most valuable resource, for many years. Recently however, Iran's economy has suffered. First, the war with Iraq created huge debts. Then, U.S. **sanctions** damaged trading, and oil prices and investments in industry fell.

**Left:** Crates and fishing nets are some of the equipment loaded onto fishing boats to help bring in the day's catch. Fishing, forestry and agriculture make important contributions to Iran's economy.

## Industry and Agriculture

Besides oil refining, Iran's main industries include petrochemicals, steel, cement and textile, car and carpet manufacturing.

Although less than half of the land in Iran is suitable for crops, more than one-third of the population works in agriculture. Wheat and barley are the country's most important crops. Farmers also produce cotton, rice, fruits, nuts, sugar beets and dairy products.

**Above:** This Iranian worker is inspecting cans of food.

# People and Lifestyle

Iran is home to many **ethnic** groups. Persians number only slightly more than half of the population. Other groups include the Lurs, Azeri, Gilaki and Mazandarani, Kurds and Arabs. **Nomadic** groups such as the Qashqai and the Bakhtiari, have lived in Iran for centuries. The Iranian government however, tries to discourage their wandering lifestyles.

**Below:** Many Iranians today can trace their roots back to the Aryan groups who came to Iran from Central Asia in the second century B.C.

**Left:** The Lurs and other minority groups live close to Iran's borders. The government wants minorities to become part of Iranian society, but some groups, especially the Kurds, have struggled for a long time to be independent.

More and more people in Iran are moving from farms and villages to cities. The cities offer greater opportunities for employment and education, as well as better health care and living conditions. About 60 per cent of Iranians now live in cities, and more than one-sixth of the total population lives in Iran's capital city, Tehran.

## Family Life

The family is at the centre of Iranian life. Family members are very close. Due to changing lifestyles, Iranian families are smaller today than in the past, but households are still large. Several generations often live together. Even when young Iranians leave home, they like to live close to their parents. Very few people live alone in Iran and

**Above:**
Family picnics are popular in Iran. This inviting picnic area is near the ancient city of Bam.

almost everyone considers marriage important. Iranians see marriage as an opportunity to expand the family.

## Marriage

Islamic law allows an Iranian man to have as many as four wives. Most men however, have only one wife. In a divorce, children stay with their father.

**Below:**
Older citizens are respected in Iranian society. Iranians believe that wisdom comes with age.

## Education

Iranians value education and have high academic standards. All Iranian children must attend school between the ages of six and fourteen. Public education is free all the way to secondary school.

Getting into an Iranian university is very difficult. Most students spend up to a year preparing for the entrance examinations. Nevertheless, more than a million Iranians currently attend institutions of higher learning. The universities in Tehran are generally considered the best.

## Religious Education

Many children in Iran attend weekly Qur'an classes taught by a Muslim religious expert called a *mullah*. Some young men go to religious schools that prepare them for **seminary** training to become a mullah.

**Below:** In most Iranian schools, girls and boys are taught separately. Boys are taught by men. Girls are taught by women.

# Religion

Ninety-eight per cent of Iran's people are Muslims. Muslims believe in one God, Allah, and that Muhammad, the founder of Islam, was Allah's last prophet. Eighty-nine per cent of Iran's Muslims are Shi'ites. Nine percent are Sunnis. Shi'ite Muslims recognise only Muhammad's descendants as rightful leaders of the Islamic world. Sunni Muslims accept other leaders.

**Below:** The area outside a mosque, the place where Muslims worship, is very busy after Friday prayers. These women are leaving a mosque in the city of Esfahan.

Two per cent of Iran's population are not Muslim. Non-Muslims are free to practise their own religions, as long as they respect Islam. Non-Muslim religious groups in Iran include Jews; Christians, who are mainly Orthodox Armenians; and **Zoroastrians**.

Iran's largest group of non-Muslims are followers of the Baha'i faith. The Iranian government however, considers this religion anti-Islamic, or against Islam. Baha'is believe that all world religions share one message and the same God.

# Language

The official language of the Islamic Republic of Iran is Persian, which is also called Farsi. Farsi developed from Middle Persian and Parthian. Written in Arabic characters, it is also used in Afghanistan. Only about half of the Iranian people however, speak Farsi as a first language. One-fourth of the population speaks Turkic languages. Other languages spoken in Iran are Kurdish, Luri, Balochi and Arabic.

**Left:** Iranians enjoy reading many types of books and newspapers.

**Left:** The tombs of thirteenth- and fourteenth-century poets Saadi and Hafez are in the city of Shiraz. Hafez's tomb is inside this small pavilion, which was built in 1953.

# Literature

Poetry is Iran's most well-known form of literature. The most famous Iranian poet known outside the country is Omar Khayyam. His *Rubaiyat*, written in the eleventh century, has been translated into English and many other languages. Two other admired Iranian poets are Saadi and Hafez.

Iranian writers often use their work to examine Iranian life and educate the public. Many writers have been punished by the government for their negative views.

# Arts

Iran's most widely known art form is handmade carpets. Throughout the world, Persian carpets are found in grand hotels, stately mansions and ordinary homes. In Iran, every home has beautiful carpets.

The carpets from each region of the country have their own distinct colours and patterns. The rich colours come

**Below:** Persian carpets are made of wool or silk that is tied by hand to a base of cotton or silk threads. High-quality carpets can have more than 1 million knots per square metre. Experienced carpet makers can tie between 10,000–14,000 knots a day.

from plant dyes. Common patterns include flowers, fruits and animals. The highest-quality carpets are made of silk.

## Miniature Paintings

Using brushes that have a single hair, Iranian artists create paintings so tiny that details often cannot be seen without a magnifying glass. The images are usually painted onto bone or leather.

# Crafts and Calligraphy

Blacksmiths, woodworkers and jewellers are some of the Iranian artists who sell their handcrafted products in Iran's bazaars, or marketplaces.

Iranian artists also use calligraphy, which is the art of elegant handwriting and lettering, to decorate everything from carpets and wall tiles to banners

**Left:** Craftspeople in Iran, such as this coppersmith, spend a long time learning a trade before being considered skilled **artisans**.

**Left:**
The mausoleum, or burial place, of Shah Nematollah Vali is an excellent example of Islamic architecture. It is located in the town of Mahan.

and paintings. Calligraphy **inscriptions** are usually inspired by the writings in the Qur'an.

## Architecture

Architecture is one of the most beautiful expressions of Iranian art. The design of most buildings in Iran include Islamic features such as domes, courtyards and **minarets**. Buildings are often decorated with white plasterwork, colourful tile designs and intricate mosaics.

# Leisure

Iranians are sociable people so they especially enjoy activities that include their families and friends. Other than visits and get-togethers, rural Iranians have very few leisure activities available to them. City dwellers however, can choose from a variety of activities.

In summer, the weather is so hot that most shops and offices close in the afternoon. People often sleep after eating lunch. In the evening, when the

**Left:** Iranians in urban areas enjoy riding bicycles and relaxing in the park. During summer, children can play in the parks until after midnight.

**Left:** Mountain resorts in Iran are popular places for skiing and relaxing. Some peaks in the northern part of the country are snow-capped all year long.

air is cooler, people like to walk, shop and eat at restaurants. Many cities have amusement parks that stay open late on summer nights.

In winter, skiing is a popular activity for people living in cities close to the mountains. For example, people from Tehran ski on the slopes of the Elburz Mountains every Friday.

# Sports

Unofficially, football is Iran's national sport. All cities have football teams and six football stadiums in Iran can seat up to 128,000 fans each.

Volleyball, table tennis, martial arts, shooting and horse riding are also popular sports in Iran. Iranians enjoy wrestling too. Wrestling events are held in gymnasiums called *zurkhaneh* which means "house of strength".

**Above:** Iran's national football team played well in the 1998 World Cup championship held in France. Iran won in the first round against the United States but then lost to Germany.

# Women and Sports

For most sports events in Iran, men and women are separated. Men can attend football matches anywhere in the country. Only recently, however, have women been allowed to attend matches in major cities. Unless women follow strict Islamic rules about clothing, they may perform sports in women-only stadiums.

**Below:** Iranian women are excellent at showjumping and other horse riding events. Islamic laws, however, make careers in sports difficult for Muslim women to pursue.

# Festivals

The Iranian New Year, called *Noruz*, has been celebrated for thousands of years. It is Iran's biggest festival, starting on the first day of spring and lasting up to two weeks.

For one month each year, Muslims celebrate *Ramazan*, or Ramadan, which is a time of fasting. All healthy adults must not eat, drink or smoke during daylight hours. At the end of Ramazan, they enjoy a feast known as *Eid-e Fetr*.

**Left:** Residents of Mahan hold an outdoor concert to celebrate the thirteenth day of Noruz, the Iranian New Year.

**Left:** On 1 April, Tehran University students celebrate the anniversary of the day Iran became the Islamic Republic of Iran.

Muslims celebrate *Eid-e Qorban*, or the Feast of the Sacrifice, about two months after Ramazan. At this time, many Muslims make a **pilgrimage** to Mecca in Saudi Arabia. Shi'ite Muslims also celebrate the birthdays of their saints.

The Iranian government allows non-Muslim religious groups to celebrate their own holidays. Easter is an important Christian festival.

# Food

Some Iranian foods are commonly found in other Middle Eastern countries but many Iranian dishes are unique. Meals usually consist of rice served with meat and vegetable stews that combine sweet and sour flavours. Soups, kebabs and omelettes are also popular in Iran. Iranian cooking uses a lot of green herbs, dried fruits and nuts and fruit pastes.

**Below:** Iran has a variety of breads, all of which are baked in clay ovens. Fresh, hot bread is available several times each day.

Many Iranians follow food rules that define all foods as either "hot" or "cold", based on how a food affects the person eating it. Hot foods include sweets and meats. Cold foods include yoghurt and fish.

## Sweets and Snacks

Iranians enjoy rice puddings and pastries, especially baklava, which has layers of crisp, paper-thin pastry dough filled with nuts and coated with sugar syrup. Favourite snacks include dried fruits and nuts.

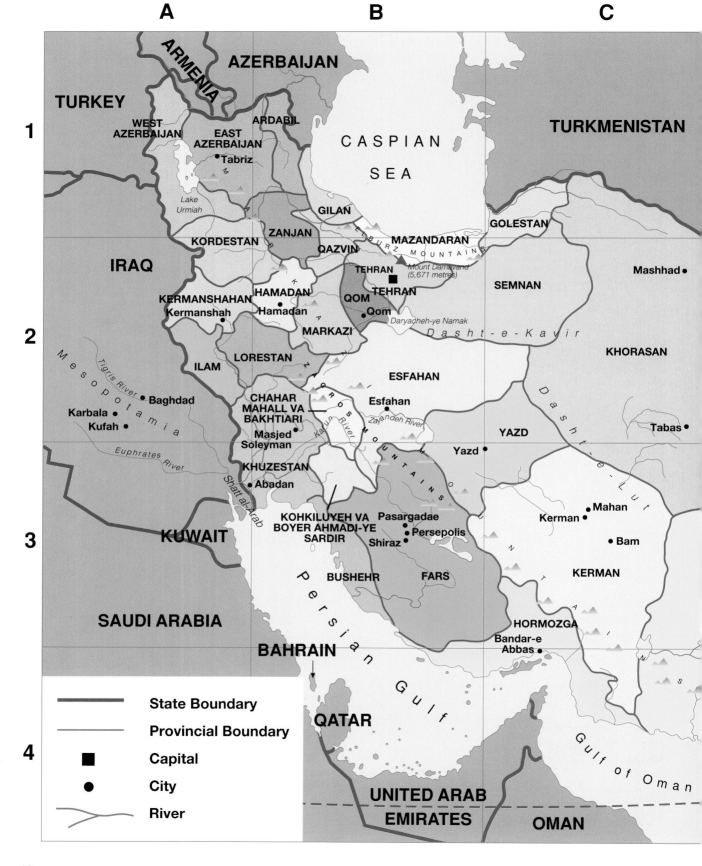

A B C

TURKEY
ARMENIA
AZERBAIJAN
1
WEST
AZERBAIJAN
ARDABIL
EAST
AZERBAIJAN
•Tabriz
CASPIAN
SEA
TURKMENISTAN
Lake
Urmiah
GILAN
GOLESTAN
ZANJAN
MAZANDARAN
ELBURZ MOUNTAINS
KORDESTAN
QAZVIN
IRAQ
KERMANSHAHAN
Kermanshah •
HAMADAN
•Hamadan
TEHRAN
TEHRAN
Mount Damavand
(5,671 metres)
SEMNAN
Mashhad •
QOM
•Qom
MARKAZI
Daryacheh-ye Namak
2
Dasht-e-Kavir
KHORASAN
LORESTAN
ESFAHAN
Mesopotamia
Tigris River
ILAM
•Baghdad
CHAHAR
MAHALL VA
BAKHTIARI
•Esfahan
Zayandeh River
YAZD
Dasht-e-Lut
Tabas •
Karbala •
Kufah •
Euphrates River
Masjed
Soleyman
Kalun River
ZAGROS MOUNTAINS
Yazd •
KHUZESTAN
•Abadan
Shatt al-Arab
KOHKILUYEH VA
BOYER AHMADI-YE
SARDIR
Pasargadae
•
Persepolis
Shiraz •
Kerman •
Mahan
• Bam
3
KUWAIT
BUSHEHR
FARS
KERMAN
SAUDI ARABIA
Persian Gulf
HORMOZGA
Bandar-e
Abbas •
BAHRAIN

State Boundary
Provincial Boundary
■ Capital
• City
River

QATAR
Gulf of Oman
4
UNITED ARAB
EMIRATES
OMAN

42

**D**

IRAN

N

AFGHANISTAN

PAKISTAN

SISTAN VA
BALUCHESTAN

*Tropic of Cancer*

Afghanistan D2–D3
Ardabil B1
Armenia A1
Azerbaijan A1–B1

Bahrain B4
Bam C3
Bushehr B3

Caspian Sea B1
Chahar Mahall va
    Bakhtiari B2

East Azerbaijan
    A1–B1
Elburz Mountains
    B1–B2
Esfahan (city) B2
Esfahan (province)
    C2–B3

Fars B3–C3

Gilan B1
Golestan C1
Gulf of Oman C4

Hamadan B2
Hormozgan
    C3–C4

Ilam A2
Iraq A1–A3

Karun River B2–B3
Kerman C3–C4
Kermanshahan A2
Khorasan C1–D3
Khuzestan B2–B3
Kohkiluyeh va
    Boyer Ahmadi-ye
    Sardir B3
Kordestan A1–B2
Kuwait A3

Lorestan A2–B2

Mahan C3
Markazi B2
Markazi Mountains
    A1–D4
Mazandaran B1–B2
Mount Damavand
    B2

Oman C4

Pakistan D3–D4
Pasargadae B3
Persepolis B3
Persian Gulf B3–B4

Qatar B4
Qazvin B1–B2
Qom B2

Saudi Arabia A3–B4
Semnan B2–C2
Shiraz B3
Sistan va
    Baluchestan
    C3–D4

Tehran (city) B2
Tehran (province)
    B2
Turkey A1
Turkmenistan
    C1–D2

United Arab
    Emirates B4–C4

West Azerbaijan A1

Yazd C2–B3

Zagros Mountains
    B2–B3
Zanjan B1–B2

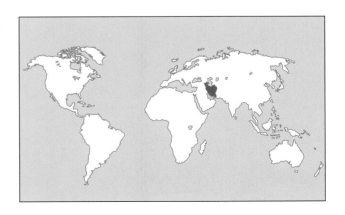

43

# Quick Facts

| | |
|---|---|
| **Official Name** | The Islamic Republic of Iran |
| **Capital** | Tehran |
| **Official Language** | Persian, or Farsi |
| **Population** | 69,018,924 (July 2004 estimate) |
| **Land Area** | 1,648,000 square kilometres |
| **Provinces** | Ardabil, Bushehr, Chahar Mahall va Bakhtiari, East Azerbaijan, Esfahan, Fars, Gilan, Golestan, Hamadan, Hormozgan, Ilam, Kerman, Kermanshahan, Khorasan, Khuzestan, Kohkiluyeh va Boyer Ahmadi-ye Sardir, Kordestan, Lorestan, Markazi, Mazandaran, Qazvin, Qom, Semnan, Sistan va Baluchestan, Tehran, West Azerbaijan, Yazd, Zanjan |
| **Highest Point** | Mount Damavand (5,671 metres) |
| **Major River** | Karun River |
| **Major Mountains** | Elburz range, Markazi range, Zagros range |
| **Main Religion** | Islam |
| **Major Festivals** | Ashura, Eid-e Fetr, Eid-e Qorban, Noruz |
| **Currency** | Rial (14,483.10 IRR = £1 in July 2004) |

**Opposite:** The Gate of All Nations is located in Persepolis.

45

# Glossary

**archaeologists:** scientists who study ancient peoples and their cultures.

**artisans:** skilled workers who create handmade crafts.

**autocratic:** having complete and unlimited power.

**circulates:** moves around or flows through from place to place.

**coronation:** the act of crowning a king, queen or other ruler.

**dynasty:** a family of rulers who inherit their power.

**elevation:** the height or altitude of a place above sea level.

**emblem:** a figure, sign or symbol that stands for an object or idea and is used to identify a person, group or nation.

**ethnic:** related to a certain race or culture of people.

**exile:** the state of being sent away by force from a person's native land.

**feudal:** related to an ancient political system in which subjects pledged their service to a lord in exchange for protection and the use of land.

**inscriptions:** words that are painted, printed or engraved on a hard surface, often as a dedication.

**juries:** groups of people selected to listen to the facts of court trials and make decisions based on law.

**minarets:** the tall thin towers attached to Muslim mosques, from which people are called to prayer.

**nomadic:** related to people who move from place to place within a region.

**persecuted:** treated cruelly and unfairly for reasons related to politics, race or religion.

**pilgrimage:** a journey made to a sacred place as an act of religious devotion.

**plateau:** a large area of high, flat land that rises sharply above the land around it.

**sanctions:** measures taken by a country to restrict trade and official contact with another country that has broken international law.

**seminary:** an institution of higher learning that trains its students to be ministers of a religious faith.

**sovereign:** of the highest rank or power.

**subtropical:** nearby or bordering the hot, damp areas closest to the equator.

**Zoroastrians:** members of a Persian religion started by the prophet Zoroaster in the sixth century B.C.

# More Books to Read

*Alexander the Great. Famous Lives* series.  Jane Bingham (Usbourne Publishing Ltd)

*Alexander the Great. Penguin Readers* series.  Fiona Beddall (Penguin)

*Kurds. Threatened Cultures* series.  John King (Hodder Wayland)

*Muslim Mosque. Where We Worship* series.  Angela Wood (Franklin Watts)

*My Muslim Year. Year of Religious Festivals* series.  Cath Senker (Hodder Wayland)

*The Seven Wise Princesses: A Medieval Persian Epic.*  Wafa Tarnowska
   (Barefoot Books)

*To the Edge of the World: The Story about Alexander the Great.*  Stewart Ross
   (Hodder Wayland)

# Web Sites

www.arabiannights.org/rubaiyat/

www.intercaspian.com

www.jamaat.org/islam

www.lexicorient.com/e.o/iran.htm


Due to the dynamic nature of the Internet, some web sites stay current longer than others. To find additional web sites, use a reliable search engine with one or more of the following keywords to help you locate information about Iran. Keywords: *Cyrus the Great, Islam, Kurds, Noruz, Persian Empire, Qur' an, Tehran.*

**Note to parents and teachers**
Every effort has been made by the Publishers to ensure that these web sites are suitable for children, that they are of the highest educational value, and that they contain no inappropriate or offensive material. However, because of the nature of the Internet, it is impossible to guarantee that the contents of these sites will not be altered. We strongly advise that Internet access is supervised by a responsible adult.

# Index